ALSO BY MÓNICA DE LA TORRE

Acúfenos
Author

Appendices, Illustrations & Notes
Co-author, with artist Terence Gower

Reversible Monuments: Contemporary Mexican Poetry
Co-editor, with Michael Wiegers

Poems by Gerardo Deniz
Editor and translator

TALK SHOWS

Mónica de la Torre

```
811.6 T635t
Torre, M´onica de la.
Talk shows
```

SWITCHBACK BOOKS
CHICAGO

Copyright © 2006 Mónica de la Torre. All rights reserved.
No part of this book may be reproduced without the permission of the publisher.

ISBN-13: 978-0-9786172-0-2
ISBN-10: 0-9786172-0-7

LIBRARY OF CONGRESS CONTROL NUMBER: 2006905845

Book design: Cathy Nieciecki
Cover art: Bruce Pearson

Switchback Books
Brandi Homan, *Editor-in-Chief*
Hanna Andrews and Becca Klaver, *Founding Editors*
PO Box 478868
Chicago, IL 60647
editors@switchbackbooks.com
www.switchbackbooks.com

ACKNOWLEDGMENTS

Grateful acknowledgment is made to the editors of the following publications in which some of these poems first appeared: *American Poet*, *BOMB*, *Boston Review*, *Chain*, *The Columbia Review*, *Failbetter.com*, *Fence*, *LIT*, *Pierogi Press*, *Superflux*, and *not enough night*. "To and No Fro" resulted from a collaboration with poet/filmmaker Abigail Child. An earlier version of "How to Look at Mexican Highways" appeared in *Circuito Interior*, a catalog of a retrospective exhibition of Silvia Gruner at the Museo Carrillo Gil in Mexico City. "Golfers in the Family" resulted in a collaboration with Bruce Pearson for the exhibition *SportsCult* at Apex Art in New York. "Driven by a Strange Desire" is featured in the anthology *Isn't It Romantic: 100 Love Poems by Younger American Poets* (eds. Brett Fletcher Lauer and Aimee Kelley, Verse Press) and in *Legitimate Dangers: American Poets of the New Century* (eds. Michael Dumanis and Cate Marvin, Sarabande Books) along with "How to Look at Mexican Highways" and "Golfers in the Family." "Texas" appeared in the chapbook *Rebel Road #3*.

Thanks to Brandi Homan, Hanna Andrews, and Becca Klaver for their invaluable insight and dedication, and to Lee Ann Brown and Cecilia Vicuña for their support.

My gratitude also goes to Mary Jo Bang, Mark Bibbins, Timothy Donnelly, Craig Dworkin, Aura Estrada, Forrest Gander, Alan Gilbert, Carolee Schneemann, Brenda Shaughnessy, Susan Swenson, Nina Subin, and Eliot Weinberger. Without their friendship and encouragement this book would not have materialized. To Bruce Pearson, my mostest.

To Catherine Spiegel, my mother

TABLE OF CONTENTS

How-Tos

- 3   The Script
- 5   For Rose to Be We Need a Celebrity
- 6   The Angel in the House
- 7   Letter from One Practitioner to Another
- 8   The Other Practitioner Writes Back
- 9   How to Look at Mexican Highways
- 11   *How to Be Well Dressed*: An Intervention

Self and Society

- 17   Durango, Durango
- 18   Migrating Birds
- 19   Driven by a Strange Desire
- 21   Aphorisms for Asthmatics
- 22   Skin Is Warm: 31 Nudes
- 24   Pattern Recognition
- 27   Bite Its Heart Until It Learns
- 28   Poem in Spanish
- 29   To and No Fro

Reality Bites

- 33   Talk Shows
- 35   Elementary Morality I
- 36   Texas
- 45   Elementary Morality II
- 46   Ne Pleonastic
- 47   Poems of Depth
- 49   On Translation
- 51   Bankrupt Books: A Collage

Fitness

55	Shadow Self
56	Convergence: A Picture Puzzle
58	Body Trends
59	Golfers in the Family
61	Table Tennis
62	Soccer Dreams
63	Demolition Derby

Notes

HOW-TOS

THE SCRIPT

I.

You thought this would be
a dance lesson,
things were easier then.
No marimbas, no clarinets;
only a longing for the fun
to begin.
Rain came down.
Nothing seems as remote
as the days you didn't
have to think about it:
always already there,
gushing out. Control
was required to stop ideas
from overflowing.
You did your job well,
you killed them as one kills
Easter baby chickens.

II.

Rasputin was on the lookout.
Magdalene had multipurpose hair:
Kumernis had it in stocks
where and when she needed it,
on her beard especially. Anything
to keep the Barbarians away
will do. Chopped noses,
rotten chicken stuffed in corsets.
We were told that the demons
would come out in Maine.
They hate recollections and certainty.
Their favorite verb is sabotage.

III.

Rasputin helps one to recognize inspiration; but, oh, what could imagination be?

To retrieve, to plunder, to forge.

To be bored.

To rip kites so they may stay on the ground.

To forget jokes and misunderstand common sense.

To sit for four hours without getting up.

To count words and people and only remember their numbers.

To listen closely to what loons could be trying to say.

To permutate dots so that lines are never identical to each other.

To return to known places and act always the same, thus the slightest change might become apparent.

To force things to happen.

To pretend there's meaning when all that comes out is a "My dog loves me and he's no showboat."

To think there's nothing to say.

To leap from canopy to can openers to can open her.

You've begun, now use your props.

FOR ROSE TO BE WE NEED A CELEBRITY

In a library with at least eleven windows
less than eleven women who knew each other not
told each other secrets
that were meant, at some point, to be public.
Who'd like to be Oprah?
When a secret comes it is not silent,
unless it's not even a secretion.
Saliva is not interchangeable with ink.
"I am purposeless," the secret cried
but words were meant to imprint themselves
on the mind of the woman whose stomach
kept making discomfiting noises.
How about Charlie?
It should have been decreed that every Friday
they tell each other secrets.
The problem was that they gathered secretly in a semicircle
and nobody was comfortable giving orders.
A voice said, "Time's up!" but it was only a voice
waiting for the minutes to elapse.
"Tell me what Sophia is thinking and I'll tell you what
Sandra's about to write," bartered Kara, to no effect.
"What fun this is, or can be," thought Jessica of telling Linda.
Billie muttered to herself.

THE ANGEL IN THE HOUSE

a) Makes a thoughtful Christmas gift.
Beware and handle with care. Boxes
may damage the wings.

And/or b) Pluck all feathers out,
rinse with lukewarm water,
let boil until
distinctive features vanish.

Customize your angel,
dress it up,
draw its face (if it doesn't already have one).

Or, c) Dissect,
wire electric installment
through spinal cord.
Hang it.

LETTER FROM ONE PRACTITIONER TO ANOTHER

    For the love of words, stop describing! If you want to go from something particular to something less frivolous stop explaining to us why you think those little steps that you took that day are relevant at all. You suffer from hyperaesthesia, we know. But let us trace the line that connects the dots. Dots speak louder. They do and fear is as irrational as an unnecessary metaphor. You know, the type computer technicians use to explain what's wrong with our machines. If you own a car and let six people drive it, something is bound to go wrong, isn't it? You get in the driver's seat and can't see a thing in the mirrors; you only notice this after you've started to drive. You try to slow down and realize that the brake pedal has lost some of its responsiveness. The machine is all fucked up. Drivers each deal with this situation differently.

THE OTHER PRACTITIONER WRITES BACK

Hey babe, Kiev love star! Rats evolve, I kebab. Yeh!

Try again.

Ne morose ode: More grow on Kiev, love star. Rats evolve, I know, or Gerome does, or omen?

Try again, open your eyes so you can look closer.

                      OJO

                    OHIO
             -          -
              -       -
               -   -
Rongi rattad ragisevad   -   Ruedan las ruedas del ferrocarril
               -   -
              -       -
             -          -
                    OIHO

HOW TO LOOK AT MEXICAN HIGHWAYS

1. You are not going anywhere.
    1.1. No one is waiting for you.
    1.2. In case someone is waiting for you, you can always explain the delay later.
    1.3. Blame it on the traffic, no one else knows that you chose to walk.

2. Don't look at the pavement, look at the things that you don't see when you're indoors.
    2.1. Water towers.
    2.2. Cables.
        2.2.1. Cables bringing other people's voices and faces onto TV monitors.
        2.2.2. Cables bringing electricity to light bulbs and refrigerators.
    2.3. Laundry on clotheslines.
    2.4. Empty cans of food.
        2.4.1. With flowers growing out of them.
        2.4.2. With cactuses growing out of them.

3. Feel the waves surrounding you.
    3.1. Waves bringing other people's voices to the speakers of your sound system.
    3.2. Waves of street sounds.

4. Measure how fast you can run up and down staircases; compare that to the speed of the cars driving by.

5. When you tire, stand in the middle of the overpass.
    5.1. Look down.
    5.2. Try to look ahead, attempt to delineate the city's skyline.
        5.2.1. If there's too much pollution, look down again.
        5.2.2. Hold on tighter to the rail.
        5.2.3. Stay there a bit longer; remember no one is waiting for you.
        5.2.4. You're not going anywhere.

6. Through the rails you will see stories unfolding on the street.
    6.1. Pay attention.
    6.2. You are not they.
    6.3. They are not they.
        6.3.1. They are one plus one plus one, indefinitely.

7. You're surrounded by monads going somewhere.

8. There is a purpose to their movement.

9. Desire is a Federacy.

HOW TO BE WELL DRESSED: AN INTERVENTION

Whenever anyone comes upon Amy Vanderbilt she is perfectly put together. "It takes time. I have to find it. Just to get my face on takes me an hour." Few women can spend this disproportionate amount of time on their personal appearance but Amy Vanderbilt has it to spare. Her intelligence and thought allow her to present herself confidently for the world's examination: a well-dressed, well-groomed product of her time. Listen to the cry of a liberated woman: "I did not throw my clothes on with a pitchfork!"

She does amazing things with scarves and pins and knows that a sense of style can be acquired. She knows that dressing well demands studious shopping, not haphazard flying trips to the stores.... It all started in her closet. One day she was ruthless and, for once, got a clear picture of her wearable wardrobe. The rest was simply eliminated.

The Life She Leads

She sits down with pencil and paper and analyzes her life. What activities fill her days? Club affairs, Scouts, PTA? She often does lunch, takes in a matinee. She holds neither a full- nor a part-time job. She's a house and garden type who enjoys a once-a-week dinner date with her husband. She chooses clothes that suit her roles in life. For renewal she considers the well-dressed women who share her activities, analyzes their costumes detail by detail, and discovers what makes them chic. Despite this, she's no carbon copy of every neighbor on the block.

In Step with Style

Amy Vanderbilt is in step with style. What does this mean to her? That she rushes right out and adopts a "new look"? She's cautious when it comes to this query, her reaction: to wait and see. A truly "legitimate" fashion trend shapes up only gradually. Its life expectancy? About three years. Fashions come and fashions go. O but the shirtwaist dress, the Chanel suit, the English tweed suit, the trench coat, and of course,

11

sweaters and skirts. Such classic clothes can always be counted on to wear and serve well. Listen to the cry of a liberated woman: "Fashion! That's my slave!"

A Color-Scheming Woman

Amy Vanderbilt has no doubt that colors have personality. She decides what colors she'll wear as if she were planning a luncheon. Blue is universally appealing, orange is exciting (although sometimes irritating), yellow is gay, green is restful, red is friendly and outgoing. Navy, unlike black, has life. Black is not a wise choice for wear in Suburbia or country. When Amy Vanderbilt wears pastels she appears sweet, simple, and girlish.

In her chart there are enough columns to include the five basic types in the mind of a white color-scheming woman: blondes, brown-eyed brunettes, blue-eyed brunettes, redheads, and those with gray hair. Thanks to her chart her eyes are open to the wonderful world of colors and what they can do to dramatize her. When shopping she plays it safe by using swatches, certain that her memories, like most people's, are color blind.

Flattering Fashions

To solve problems that are strictly figurative she relies on do and don't tips. Since she has a full figure she wears clothes with vertical details that carry the eye up and down rather than across her figure. She avoids square and sweetheart necklines, shiny fabrics such as satin and clinging ones such as chiffon. No chokers, scarves, or bibs for the short-necked!

When Amy Vanderbilt spends seasons in the sun she's not allowed to shed her girdle: it's hot and uncomfortable but wearing it is the price she must pay for not counting calories with care. She often goes to the beach, so she doesn't hesitate to wear a jacket over her blessed Lycra suit to camouflage bulges when she's not in the swim.

Travel Plans

Once she spent 24 pre-jet hours in planes and at airports as she and her husband headed from New York to Cairo, where she was to meet her husband's family for the first time. Imagine facing this sort of meeting in a dress she's literally slept in! But it was a knit and nary a wrinkle showed as she stepped out the plane at 6:30 a.m. (Cairo time)! Among other basics, she took with her a well-stocked cosmetic travel kit, a hat to wear when visiting churches, and a suit, handy for what the natives term an "unheard-of cold spell at this time of the year." Listen to the cry of a liberated woman: "I'm not weighed down with luggage containing clothes I'll never wear!"

Personal Appearances

Unaccustomed as she was to public speaking, there came a time when she had to step into the spotlight and introduce a guest speaker. She concentrated glamour in a smart-looking hat but made sure it sat securely on her head, it was free of wild-waving feathers and flowers that flounced every time she moved a muscle. Listen to the cry of a liberated woman: "I choose jewelry that provides no sound effects!"

SELF AND SOCIETY

DURANGO, DURANGO

There once was a weeping willow that never wept. Maybe someone missed the weeping, or the tree just looked like it was grieving but it wasn't because there was no reflecting pool below it.

This is how one who has a story can begin a story. When one does not have a story one can write a letter, for instance.

>Dear Papa,
>
>I imagine you on your sailboat, drinking a beer and thinking about the splendid life you've got now that you keep fewer houses. I miss your Sunday sense of humor. I think about it constantly.
>
>   Love,
>
>   Moi
>
>PS: Perhaps you and I could talk over the phone one of these days, about why the only time you've ever mentioned your hometown was when you told us the story about the locals burning down a set for a Western so as to heat their tortillas? Like you, I'm afraid of sounding trite when I talk about local flavor. Is that why I've got no story? There's a big lake here that you might find attractive. You could practice your water sports while I remember the right spelling for lacunae.

MIGRATING BIRDS

Victor gets a real sense of power
from making his own raisins. He buys
pounds and pounds of grapes
and leaves them to dry
on the kitchen table.

Theresa doesn't want to hear about
her ex-husband's cancer. Not on Father's Day.
She takes a train all night
to have breakfast with her cousin.
All Sunday she rides the train back.

Once Martin's wife had left,
he decided to take advantage of her space.
He built a sauna where her closet was,
and now sits there every morning
to read the paper and Buddha.

One night Helga wore her prettiest dress,
though she knew he wouldn't be there.
She drank dry white, got drunk
(she was on a diet), and fell down.
Later he saw the holes in her pantyhose.

María was usually bumping into
furniture. Each time she got closer to what
she wanted. "What do you want from me?"
"Nothing," he replied, so she took off
and felt like migrating birds. But many.

DRIVEN BY A STRANGE DESIRE

I. Before breakfast

When the sun turns gray and I become tired
of looking at your multicolored shoes

I will give you balloons for all the holes
we speak too much to fill. Who believes

in air, nowadays? Or do you prefer tea
with the dried fruit I will have to throw out

the window of your room? Because I want
this to stop I want this to stop I want this

II. Toward the Moors in Spain

To kill dragons is a different thing
in my family there are only lizards.

In Sevilla—never famous for its lamps—
a dissected crocodile hangs from a roof.

The reptile, the Crown's Byzantine gift. Its teeth
suspended in the air of the cathedral.

I stole a pair of shoes, but didn't run far
from the orchard where water had women's scent.

Thirst is not fear, thirst is not green, but has wings
like dragons, or airplanes. As oranges

in Sevilla, driven by a strange desire
to stay where they are. Floating. Suspended.

III. Toward Virgo

The Milky Way is not only expanding;
the Bang is not only a bang. It is drifting

and being pulled away from, let's say, something.
Because dark matter is ninety-nine of what

there is and visible matter is so small
it clusters together and forms a Great Wall.

China and Spain and my eyes reading the paper.
We are still together, are we not, wondering if.

APHORISMS FOR ASTHMATICS

*

"Are you afraid of death?" Answer the doctor's first question with a question. His reply: "Have you got issues with authority?"

*

Unoxidized thoughts. Hope not to wake anyone while you feel you're dying. Try not to make a racket.

*

Asthma can be literary. Carpentier always had wheezing in his novels. Baroque counterpoint: as characters came to life, one died.

*

There once was a croaking lizard. *The feild was odious Quhair dragouns, lessertis, askis, edders swatterit.*

*

Suggestions: sleep like in the Middle Ages, at a right angle. Or at least try to. Worry not, choking reveals the truest you.

SKIN IS WARM: 31 NUDES

I. The Frame

II. The Drawings

An improvised destiny, your head. (Arm carrying suitcase.)
I wish you would stop staring. (Man with a face.)
Touch me. (Dressed.)

(Reclined.) Simple.
Flesh and blood do not make. (Ink stains on paper.)
(Bow tying bun.) I am fine.

        The door is falling apart. (It wanted to get out.)

The dance has begun.
If a man were a nose. (A podium.)
What would happen if I had color. (Dark hair.)
I will have to stay here, looking at you looking at me. (Clothes lying
   on the floor.)
Almost like being alone.

        I know you want me to say something. (Thick black ink
          silhouette.)

I feel big, a body.
As a whore I will dress. (Comfortable on chair.)
Irreverence is no young shape.
I will find myself longing. (Flowery scarf.)
My leg is dissolving.

What is present. (Holding suitcase.)
My bosom, tranquil. (A florid spread.)

Asleep I am all. (She stretches.)
I wake. (A question.)
To see the world from a bed.
If I could cover my face with one finger.
Or be. (Flower in hair.)

I am many. (Seen from behind.)
Black is white. (Placid turning.)
I will lie.
We are not different. (Face with a stain.)

PATTERN RECOGNITION

Which lover from China was she trying to forget,
thinking about animals' ability to register events.
Did they realize they were being held captive?
Someone asks about a suture.

    so strong is this hunger for pattern

Do we all see fragments of the sun burning?

Clouds for reallocation.
Picture your bed,
picture the city's empty Tuesday morning beds,
how they absorb the warmth of personal belongings.

Do we all see fragments of the sun burning?

You become the bed you sleep in.

    that we see it even when it isn't there

At night there is a silence of bottled sleeping pills
(an aunt takes them to forget her husband
running away with the youngest of all spheres).

In this silence distilled
she arrives
an apple to the ground
she falls and lands solid:
someone's island mind.

(No movement at all.)
Collective injuries,
divided infinite triangles.
A hallway
breathes, pulsates,
wants to become the chambers it connects.

Home is where the heart lies
burning, an icon
of past homes burning.
A red sacrifice, an uncertain
pain of building, not fleeing.

The virgin of solitude,
a black tear stains her cheek:
Dignity.

What's so fearful about that blossom?
Its absent ligature, its lack of hesitation.

There is the true dignity that a suitcase keeps,
or an ashtray: if only a Greek statue could grow.

Don't weep,
may you be granted wings to rise above this ugliness.
I'll be pretty for father
(a father is coming to visit).

so strong is this hunger for pattern

Some souvenirs pierce the space where daily thoughts fit organized.

A sunflower stares
from the corner of a room
or it could be a sister's mouth
commanding one to open.
I fall into it,
so dumb and complicated.

There's a medium in all things one has possessed
linking one's breath to the past.

Is it always so humid when the seasons change.

If she really wanted to forget she would have to get rid of the painting.

(Cloris loved Zephyrus
because he was never around
to see the flowers wilt.)

(Zephyrus loved Cloris
because he was never around
to see the flowers wilt.)

        that we see it even when it isn't there

The wisest knows it is never a goodbye,
or else it is always.

A tree is being taken elsewhere in a truck big enough for its roots.

BITE ITS HEART UNTIL IT LEARNS

One doesn't know a thing about what poets, the blind, hookers,
call "mystery." Nada. One can't say anything.

My chest then my heart my senses in my chest
your mouth your lips your teeth your tongue.
The earth will keep on spinning in its precise orbit.
The earth that is the earth and the sky like the rose rose but stone.

Conscience is bitterness. A tragic concept.

Never did the sky have as many roads as this one.
The road becomes diluted in the desolate shadow.

Some words have the shade of a tree.
When all the meat isn't meat anymore, nor the soul,
let's return to the silence of words that come from silence.

She didn't know how to dress, so she was undressed.
A scream, at eleven, looking for a policeman.

Look at my hands: transparent like light bulbs.
That ray of light moving toward the bottom of the water.

Between us and this century
there will be free association of ideas
despite our format.

I don't think I betray my principles
if I say without bad intentions
that you have to have an ostrich stomach
to swallow such filth.
I bet nobody dares
drink a cup of holy water.

POEM IN SPANISH

The grave has more power than the eyes of the beloved.
An open grave with all its magnets.
This weight on the wings. The sky is waiting for an airship.

I have the feeling that I haven't got much life left.
Three hours after the celestial attack.

Why don't I respond when I'm being offended?
Because my religion doesn't allow me to.
Exterior maps: geography. Interior maps: psychography.
And in your hard cathedral I kneel.
Mountains pass camels pass
like the history of wars in antiquity.

Of all the men I am, I can't find any of them
without the control of the intruding eye.
Problems. Mysteries that fasten themselves to my chest.
All I want is not to see businesses nor gardens
nor markets nor eyeglasses nor elevators.

In order to serve all radio listeners,
without discriminating between social classes, I speak a tongue
that fills hearts with the law of communicating clouds.
I have my brain or whatever it is full of skull moths.
For the world to go on being what it is it must
—per force— take another form.

True poems are fires. When something cherished burns
instead of the fireman I call, rushes forth the incendiary.
It says: live, live, live!
It is Death.

TO AND NO FRO

In order of appearance

Adjective 1	Devoted
Verb 1	Endure
Noun	Walls
Adverb	Never
Adjective 2	Incestuous
Article	An
Adjective 3	Pregnant
Verb 2	Burst
Cameo appearances	Ghost wearing cat eyeglasses

Plot summary

To help her poor parents, she accepts to
to have at least someone in her life to
to teach their son a lesson, her husband is compelled to
to escape from his mean father, her son had to

                              the ghost runs away with her son,
                                   takes a bus to the country

to return the kid to his parents, an engineer drives to
to thank him, they want him to
to return their hospitality, in turn the engineer has them over to
to pass time while her tardy husband returns, she & the engineer start to

(a trio of drunks in the background intones ¿*De qué sirve querer con todo el corazón?*)

A few months later
to break free from her oppressive situation, she's willing to
to avoid causing her ailing husband a heart attack, she's forced to
to appease her guilty conscience & to make her family happy too
to move on, the engineer goes to
to to to

                                          caught in an embrace,
                                the ghost strangles her husband

Twenty years later
(Waltz at the graduation party, later the sight of empty bottles
& food platters)

                                the ghost dances mambo at the party
                                      with a beautiful young woman

to deliver bad & good news, a notary public comes to
to show love for the son he never met, the engineer bequeaths to
to avenge the older brother for rejecting her, the nurse says to
to confirm the rumors, he stays up to
to punish his mother, he tears up what to
to to to

                                    the ghost slaps the son, & says
                                  dile adiós a tu mamacita, desgraciado

the husband dies, one son marries, another goes to
to remember her beloved, she is destined to
to knit, sit facing the photograph, to

                                        the ghost dances the cha-cha,
                                          suffocates, collapses

                    La viuda emparedada, en par y da y da,
                          claustrofílica, contoured
                        immured, the double widow,
                          windowless, without.

REALITY BITES

TALK SHOWS

–Sometimes when we go out to dinner I notice that my wife doesn't respond to the things I'm saying. She seems to be listening, but doesn't answer my questions. Then I realize that she's overhearing the conversation at the table next to us.

–Get away from me! Who do you think you are, hitting my arm like that! What kind of a person are you? A terrorist?

–Don't look at me as if I was a woman with a rotten tooth, look at me as if I was me.

–¡Viva México cabrones!

–I can't think of anything I'd like to do less than to go to Disney with my dad.

–When are they going to start using electric cars, huh? It's totally idiotic. Gridlock, all the way from First Avenue! Something's wrong, you gotta change it! Damn!

–That other guy, he fell asleep while driving. He hasn't been able to work again. His whole body is covered in metal casts and stuff.
–Thirty years old!
–Y le dije, "Don't you care about yourself?" He answered no. "Well, you should care about the other drivers." Se quedó callado.

–See that ring over there? The amber one? It looks as if it has bugs in it, or crocodiles.

–Eso está más podrido que la mierda.

–I told her, "Look, I don't know you very well, but don't you think that before you leave him you should at least have a conversation with him?"

–Mom, someone told me that when you're fifteen you feel that you're in love but it's not real.

–Hey, long time no see! How's it going?
–Don't ask. Just got out of jail.
–You got lucky, Mom. Just think if I hadn't had those forty bucks on me.

–I swear, I haven't gotten a cold in fifteen years. People talk to me,
 I stay away.
–That's got to be a nice safety net, mentally.

–I've never seen so much polishing in my life.

–The walls were so thin I could hear the conversations next door. All
 women's residencies look exactly the same.
–The wall is so gross, it looks as if something's growing on it. Did you
 make it look that way?
–It's just wallpaper.

–So, if you do get to talk to someone, I need to know what she died of
 and where, who survived her, and why she was so private about her
 personal life. Then I could write an obituary.

–This so beautiful I don't find it inspiring.
–Have you been to Maine?
–Never.
–Moose are so big they couldn't fit in this room.
–Yeah, I saw some moose on television.

ELEMENTARY MORALITY I

progressive curses	performance addiction happy self-loathing	applause anxiety
unbearable clowns	fulfilled perfectionists narcissistic dorks	sleeping paranoiacs
over-protective toddlers	neglected parents delusional remedies	prescribed adults
	which pills, doctor, do you recommend to sleep at night, get up from the grass, control my erections, smile in pictures?	
squeaky seals	gnarling feast myopic brutes	clapping music

TEXAS

1. A man walks into a diplomatic agency. He finds a woman who will listen to what he needs. "Great teeth," he remarks. So she closes her mouth and asks what she can do for him. He needs cheap dental work in a foreign country. Medicare had sent him to a clinic where they destroyed a great job they had done for him in Hungary. Now he wants to know how to find a good dentist south of the border.

Desire dents

Denotes duration, drifts.
Darts downwards,
dashes during dusk, dabbles during daybreak.
Dentures denounce despair.

2. Mind your own business. The phrase must mean that there are matters exclusively mine. Maybe.

More melatonin

Mourning my mother missed much matter. Meandering morosely, muttering morning music.

Mistaken: mother meant mauve mask.
Mirrors mean much more. My mind mishandles minutiae.

3. Point fingers, fingers reeking of an utter lack of self-doubt, fingers sure of the direction of their judgments.

Farcical foes

Futuristic freaks, flaky followers,
fantastical felons.
Fast foods, fat fingers, flukes, flimsy fabrics.

4. The bride would wear a dress with considerable back and front cleavages that could only look good with a tan. She wasn't pleased with the results she got at the first tanning salon, so she visited another one. She was running out of time and still hadn't gotten the desired color. The third session that week took place on her wedding day. She died that night, never knowing her insides were baking.

Bliss

Being blurred,
becoming boundary,
bringing.

5. A man writes "Accident Reports." He's asked to send them to an editor, and when he does, a fraction of the first page accidentally gets lost. The reports are translated into another language. The accidents during transmission created "reports" that became less fact and more fiction. If there were a reason why the words fact, fiction, and fraction, begin with an "f," then we would have to admit that the fact that the alphabet starts with alpha is not accidental.

Ask

Ants about accomplishing assignments.
About arrows, about abundance.
Answers? All agree, assent, allow assuring arguments,
avoid antagonism, align.
Adversaries abound, always another, always adjustable.

6. Why isn't yellow the color of yes, why is it red? Yellow means caution. And yes? Yelling yes means no.

Yet yours

Your yearning youthful years, your yard.
Yield. Yonder, you.

7. Honestly, when we say this word the only truth we exhibit is that we'd rather be shielded by the comfortable illusion that intimate confessions bind people together. Hints dissolve.

Humanizing hoax

Holidays haven't happened haphazardly.
How hope hastens humans, hides hindrances, highlights humor.

8. An exercise in futility, could there be more of an oxymoron?

X-rated x-rays.

9. Does a swan quack? Geese honk, but this bird was certainly not a goose. It was a swan, a querulous one protecting its nesting mate. We could have been caught in the quagmire. A goose feather makes a quill, not a swan's.

Questions, queries?

Quaint qualities quench quandaries.
Quirky queens quibble quantities.
Quit quarreling, quiet!

10. Weird is the word under which current wonders are filed. Worthier than that is the fact that once the weird were witches with divination powers. They warned. For the most part, they were women.

When	*Who*	*What*	*Why*
whenever	water	waste	want
while	willows	weeping	waver
Wednesday	women	wandering	whim
wayward	whisper	wreck	wrong

11. Keep track of your expenses, keep your sense of humor, keep fallen teeth, keep in touch with your friends, keep birthday cards, keep food in the icebox, keep taking care of yourself, keep looking for the scrap of paper, keep your pets company, keep your mouth shut, keep your house clean, keep lists, keep trying.

Kissless

Knowingly karaoke-kids knicked knobs, kidnapped kinks, kicked,
knocked kettles, knickknacks.
Knock knock, keyhole.
Kitchen knives killed kneeling kings, kinetic kingdoms.

12. Both pools and pillows could resemble parenthesis, being contraptions devised to suspend. They pause the plot and distantly remind one of parents.

Pupils promoted

Passing, prone. Pursuing pastimes,
partial parenthood, paradise.
Poor people.

13. There are two reasons why one would do something: because it's an order, because it's not. Apart from that, there are questions about whether who gives the order is oneself or not, how much opposition the obligation engenders, and whether the overseer is as organized as to keep track of the completion of the order.

Ostrich

Omen: occult organ okay.
Obstacles originated, O ostrich, oversights.
Ontological organism,
old omissions only open on occasions.

14. Jabbering away one night she told her partner that without having seen the film "Raging Bull," she had chosen to name one of the characters in her "Cardio-Boxing" story "Raging John." The story was loosely based on an actual boxing class she took on Mondays. Just after she had been jabbering, she happened to find out that a friend of hers knew the man that she had named Raging John in her story. John had been in boxing classes for eleven years, and was a remarkably soft-spoken professional gemologist. Could jewels and jabs be more removed?

Just joking

Jaded juniors, jovial jerks, junkies
jostling jagged jewelry.
Judges justify jackasses.
Jarring juxtapositions, jinxed jots.

15. He was a very sophisticated person and had a superlative, far from Victorian, nose. His comments during conversation veered from his posing naked for a vanity magazine featuring attractive fifty-year-olds, to a problematic vasectomy, the generalized adversity toward his valiant views, and the usage of valedictory verbs.

Ventriloquist's victims

Vacillating
                        vagabonds
vicarious
                        vanguardists
vehement
                        vegetarians
venomous
                        vindicators

16. When do we hear noise and when can we not listen to it? Not a question to be answered, since once an annoyance is identified it's nearly impossible to nullify it. To neutralize it we make more noise: we create it, give it an intention. Noise is noisier.

> *Narrow nests*
>
> Nobody, none.
> Neither nasturtiums nor nightingales.
> Nomads named netherworlds,
> named never,
> not nuisances, no.

17. Giving she found more to give, she gave so much and so joyfully that people surrounded her not because they wanted what she gave but because they wanted to see her crumble, break apart, become rude, have an outburst of anger for those times when she couldn't not give.

> *Gimmicky Grandma*
>
> Garnished, gave grandchildren goodies, grappled grown-ups,
>   grew grass.
> Garrulous gowns gave Grannie goodlooks.
> Ghastly gargles. Gurgling gargoyles.

18. Are coincidences coincidental? Could we be powerful enough (or too aloof not to realize) that there are things being placed before our eyes just so we can see them? Even events that are bound to happen rely on a chain of unrecordable events, some of them unpleasant.

> *Chaos, confusion*
>
> Can Carmen count charitable contributions?
> Candles, canvases, comforting cakes?
> Can't currency consist?
> Concluding centuries cause commotion.

19. Exclamation points are the most overused punctuation marks in e-mails. Repetitively, we pretend that we're talking to someone and we emphasize an emphasis to make a mood come across. No matter how hard we may try, or how much we believe we've succeeded, we're still by ourselves facing a screen that does nothing by itself other than occasionally sleep.

Erotomania

Enveloped earnings,
esteemed elation,
ergo egomania, ever earnest.

20. This was a man who had a reputation for making a living by winning contests sponsored by radio stations. He listened to radio shows all day and had figured out exactly when to start calling, using speed dial. With injured fingers, his was the fastest response. Four-in-a-row, remember-this-tune: his religion.

Racing rapidly

Restless rambling resists rigor.
Relaxed relatives roam randomly.
Run, recede, reappear, regret. Return.
Radical reactions recommended,
remorseless rejections.

21. He was a bizarre character who tried to figure out how many zippers go up and down per second in his block, then he zoomed out to the whole city, the country, American continent, and so on.

Zenith

Zealous zoning.

22. To have to wait too long will increase our longing for what we long for. Notice how the longing lingers, how the letter stretches upward, lifting.

   Licking licorice

   Let loving lovers lay lazily, lion-like.
   Loyal; less letters last longer.

   Lynch lecherous liars, linking lonelinesses.
   Liars loosen lace, lend little.
   Landowners' lawns look lost, like laws.

   Larceny looms: language.

23. Couldn't anything qualify as unica? The toothbrush with which Ana Mendieta brushed her teeth the day she would be hurled out the window onto the cool pavement, her tombstone. The gun with which Valerie shot Andy Warhol. The telephone on which the news about the car crash was received. The glass that the failed artist who went on to become real famous drank water from before he hung himself. The rope, the undershirt. The typewriter in which the word hapax was typed.

   Under

   Unique unit, usual unifier.

24. Ignorance.

   Irksome issues

   Increasingly intrigued, insufficiently informed,
   individuals irrationally invest
   in Internet. Illusory innovators,
   immersed in I's, in infantile interests.
   Issue is interior infuriation, if.

25. On Sunday they took out the singing bowls. Strange, how they wouldn't sound, sometimes, and then, all of a sudden, they sung. With a wooden stick, they would surround the rim faster and faster until the brass sang.

> *Sabotage*
>
> Slowly soften stiff surfaces, study severity.
> See, specify, separate.
> Silently steal something, strike.

26. To have to.

> *Trigger*
>
> Trapped tourists
> thanked think tanks that took the time to turn the tables.
> Then they tried transforming thrills, tangential things, to totality.

ELEMENTARY MORALITY II

heaping night	rattling sheets insomniac lists	ruffled clock
jittery pillow	inept tatters talking thoughts	superfluous legs
sleepless perspective	awry condition dull gaze	inflated morning

                            over the streets
                            the shrubs out the window
                            the buildings
                            over the people
                            pushing their little feet
                            into the subway claiming
                            their single want

indifferent sleep	spatial quota jammed sequence	vanishing day

NE PLEONASTIC

There are certain constructions, however, in which *ne* is pleonastic (superfluous). In these cases *ne* has no grammatical meaning and does not negate the verb.

1) Pleonastic *ne* is often found

   a) In a clause following a comparison:

   > Their family ties weren't stronger than they didn't think they were.

   b) In connection with the following conjunctions, which take the subjunctive;

   > Had she been able to deny she hadn't refused to follow the order no one would have believed her.

   c) With verbs of doubt used negatively or interrogatively;

   > There might be no reason to get jumpy; aren't the floorboards stable?

2) A second element of negation will make the sentence negative;

   > *A moins que vous ne trouviez rien…*
   > Unless you find nothing…

3) Other expressions of fear follow the same pattern:

   > Lost in the fear of losing what hadn't been had; missed the opportunity, truly did.

   > *Je crains qu'il ne soit à l'heure.*
   > I am afraid he may be on time.

POEMS OF DEPTH

> For Gerardo Deniz, after his "20,000 Places Under Our Mothers,"
> based on Jules Verne's *20,000 Leagues Under the Sea*

I.

O Ned your name is Land and it's not anywhere near you
you're free in your captivity, holy paradox!
You tire of walking around the submarine,
of looking out at the luminous waters,
brimming with the phosphorescent zoophytes, tiny noctilucae, starfish, and aurelias
you know not how to classify.
You're bored with the sea breeze and the occasional horizon.
O harpooner, how did you land here where the only bread is a replacement, breadfruit?
What creatures are you shooting in your mind?
How you manage to stop the hand, and instead reach for the diving suit.

II.

The crew members hush when the captain's right hand comes in
                              Nemo knows he's no one;
                    he enforces, forces.

Is he a double, or an appendage?
The closest of them all.
And if the captain were left-handed?
He says, "Less paradigmatic,"
more so, more so.

The reign underwater is vertical.
Conseil hears the master's cry and immediately asks
   "Has it bitten you, Monsieur?"

"I'd pay with a limb to own the treasure I just found."
The cannibals throw stones; destroy it.
Destroy the left-handed shell, growing awkward against the clock.

Aronnax takes this lightheartedly; water being less dense,
certainly. He'll plunge. Nemo hears no news about the incident.

III.

There'll be more expeditions coming up. They'll be under, not above.
In the beds of Coral Kingdom,
the Anglo-Saxon crew member will forever dream of poinsettias, of cold
   Christmases.
His humor won't be dry, for sure.
He had managed to learn that unrecordable language, and died with it.
And it'd been so long since he'd eaten raw vegetables.
The propeller caught his hair; echoes of his hollering reverberate.

ON TRANSLATION

Not to search for meaning, but to reenact a gesture, an intent.

As a translator, one grows attached to originals. Seldom are choices so purposeful.

At midday, the translator meets with the poet at a café at the intersection where for decades streetwalkers and cross-dressers have lined up at night for passers-by to peruse.

Not a monologue, but an implied conversation. The translator's response is delayed.

The translator asks, the poet answers unrestrictedly. Someone watches the hand movements that punctuate the flow of an incomprehensible dialogue.

They're speaking about the poet's disillusionment with Freud.

One after another, vivid descriptions of the poet's dreams begin to pour out of his mouth. There's no signal of irony in his voice. Nor a hint of astonishment, nor a suggestion of hidden meanings, rather a belief in the detritus theory.

"Se me aparece un gato fosforescente. Lo sostengo en mis brazos sabiendo que no volveré a ser el mismo."

"Estoy en una fiesta. De pronto veo que el diablo está sentado frente a mí. Viste de negro, lleva una barba puntiaguda y un tridente en la mano izquierda. Es tan amable que nadie se da cuenta de que no es un invitado como los otros."

"Anuncian en la radio que Octavio Paz leerá su poema más reciente: 'Vaca… vaca… vaca… vaca… vaca… vaca… vaca…'"

"Entro a un laboratorio y percibo aromas inusitados. Aún los recuerdo."

The translator knows that nothing the poet has ever said or written reveals as much about him as the expression on his face when he was asked to pose for a picture. He greets posterity with a devilish grin. To the translator's delight, he's forced to repeat the gesture at least three or four times. The camera has no film.

BANKRUPT BOOKS: A COLLAGE

Sister

An old trick,
TV viewers think to themselves,
a chain of skits,
it's all concealed,
the lion's hunter: who brought me milk?

George,
man of sleazy shoes,
lazy bum,
self-destructive loser?

Beetles of a sinking moon,
from the beginning of times
the potato generation?

The liberator of Azkaban?

Bridget Jones? Stupidity's limit.

Talk shows:
days after days of oblivion
the stories of a death penalty administrator,
ridiculous accounts of beguiling idiocy.

Where they don't belong: Mediterranean sun,
orange trees, ocean…
The art of dullness:
Sundays on a couch.

A retrograde rock star.
The celebrity speaks…
feeding on refuse for optimum decay.
Decomposing body, decrepit mind.
Sabotage monogamy.

Stars! An evaluation of self-hate!

Have an awful time, Beowulf.

FITNESS

SHADOW SELF

Cardio-boxing kept it under control, or so I thought.
I bumped into other shadow selves though. When

the instructor accidentally punched my nose, I knew
I was no model for him. My chronic hesitancy

put him on edge, to say the least. *Use your head!*
he'd holler, making sure that he directed his gaze

toward someone other than the person to whom
he'd addressed the command. He hated being spoken to

in Spanish. His features displayed no trace of his lineage:
the only thing he looked like was an Argentine dogo.

*I've got Irish, American, German, Spanish, Mexican,
and perhaps also Marrano blood, you prick.*

Forgive me for not believing in the afterlife of tattoos.
Now that I practice water sports my shadow self

comes to the surface more often. Especially if I read
15th and 16th century Inquisition processes.

In between the lines I picture myself chopping
a couple of her fingers off. Sometimes her eyelashes

are also sliced away by the slick paring knife
we keep in our kitchen. I can't but punish her

for having bad thoughts. Last week, wearing
four-inch stilettos, I tumbled down the wooden

staircase outside of the apartment of someone
whose talent and intelligence she pretends to respect.

CONVERGENCE: A PICTURE PUZZLE

A poem is a video by Vito Acconci seducing the viewer

while showing us a close-up of his face
              Approach to Solving Puzzles (p. 253)
and trying to fit his whole body into a frame.
              —Now, when I was excavating a heap left by the mound builders…
How does a body fit on a page.
              —Excellent busts from ancient Rome!
One reads mindless of the eye movement
              Correct solution: Gainsborough. Pedestals are called in sculptural
that strings letters into sounds
              and architectural terminology "gaines." The heap left by the builders
which only make sense when emitted.
              is a "burrow." Answer: Gaines Burrow.
Released they reassemble

someone else's unspoken thoughts.
              Original 18th century jigsaw puzzles were dissected maps.
This takes place while one inadvertently
              Challenging adult puzzles peaked in the 1900s, coming in boxes
(the better the read)
              with misleading titles and no guide pictures. During the Depression
suppresses bodily sensations
              they replaced outside entertainment, restaurants and nightclubs.
—this is what immersion means.
              Then came free advertising puzzles, easier to assemble.
Where is the poem's mouth.
              After the war the industry declined.
How many feet does it have.

A piece of writing is no walkie-talkie,
              Approach to Solving Puzzles (p. 257)
and sitting alone is, at least to me,
              —Let's steal the old boy's notes on craniometry!

not very conducive.
    —I beseech you not to.
There's a word.
    Correct solution: The Virginian. "To steal" is of course, to "thieve."
What if the hand of the reader
    The lad on the left tries to urge his companion not to. The point
were required to assemble a "sense,"
    indicated on the skull is the "inion." Answer: Thieve Urge Inion.
unlike the tiny figure of the skier on the lake

that got in the way of my thoughts
    In 1965 came "the world's most difficult puzzle": Pollock's
and makes no sense except for forcing
    Convergence, No. 10. Hundreds of thousands of Americans
my eyes to move about non-linearly.
    struggled to assemble it. "Jungle-like assemblies of the dripped
This is the first step.
    line in brilliance of color." "Glowing colors melt and merge
You might suspect by now that it is summer
    into a massive over-all effect that is both intimate and elusive."
and that instead of writing, I'd rather be sunbathing.
    "A progressive abandonment of forethought; a leaving things
Who doesn't love to have a good time.
    to chance." "He said he'd stand on his painting."
I crushed an insect, its blood is on the page.
    "Personalized skywriting."
It was probably mine anyway.

Poor little red bug that knew not
    Something like the wallpaper in Al Ruppersberg's *Nabokov's Room*,
how to leave the page,
    a double-sided puzzle.
afraid of the abruptness of its edges.

I'm torn: to write and not to swim?

BODY TRENDS

The world is everything that is the staircase.
Up and down, kicking snow off their feet,

climbing two steps at a time, hopping a bit
to feel, for a short span, in control. StairMaster,

what will it be today? Shall we test for endurance,
resistance or strength? The sky's the limit

for the social climbers. Choosing to practice
their skills in small-scale situations, they climb

84 floors in 20 minutes. Social climbers know
that dropping the right name at the right time

might open a door. Nothing makes one feel better
than the praise that they can come up with when

in need of the same treatment themselves. Dependent
on downward comparison, social climbers are loyal

to those who will always be up. They use words like
magnificent and splendid, and will go out of their way

to never look desperate. Nothing bothers them more
than the nearby climbers going up faster than they.

They're looking out to the future ahead, and miss
the sign on the control panel of the Textrys II:

Caution: Stop climbing if you don't feel good!

GOLFERS IN THE FAMILY

A Brit exclaims, "O to build character in a playground riddled with hazards! O gusts of wind, bumpy treeless fairways, deep bunkers, knee-high rough!"

Golf should be played by the seashore was the dictum Scots received from Nature. They have been much relieved to find this in accord with their Calvinist beliefs. Man is meant to suffer; never more than when he goes out to enjoy himself.

Despite his preference for courses designed to penalize players who stray from the path from tee to green, an American claims, "Games ought not to be played in moral gymnasiums: give me vistas, decorative ponds, token fairway bunkers!" (Far more than anybody else, Americans have found hanging watercolors of golf courses in the bathrooms of their homes in good taste. The choice of WalMart's interior decorators to have them enliven restrooms must also have been informed by this longing for pastoral environments.)

As in other developing countries, in Chinese boomtowns the real business deals are done while playing golf. (Some test potential partners by playing with them first.) If in China the way of doing business is lubricated by guanxi, in Mexico, for instance, it's lubricated by the drinks the caddy helpfully provides. (By the way, certain circumstances allow for betting to be considered business.)

Whatever one's nationality is one mustn't forget the ancient maxim: *Forget length when you're in a bunker from hell; make sure you get out of it before you get ambitious.*

Wives and daughters of golfers around the globe identify with their being excluded from the game; they either don't understand the language of golf or they speak it with far too much trepidation. They like that their men are out facing hazards, the familiarity between tea and tee, and the fraternal spirit of the handicap system.

(Another aside: It is not infrequent for some women to picture men naked when they feel harassed by them. In their minds, men almost immediately lose their threatening power. Some men feel naked at the golf course, their weaknesses far from concealed. Golf outfits spell overcompensation.)

Those who nervously flick remote controls tend to oversee the intended poetry of this far from telegenic game. Any player would sustain that more than any other sport, the aim of the game—to complete the course in the fewest possible strokes—looks infinitely easier than it is.

Like courses themselves, the history of the game has been non-linear. Main controversies have involved, unsurprisingly, the introduction of technological advances into the game. Rubber-core balls were considered nearly prosthetic when they first appeared in 1898. Those who excelled at playing with the Indian gutta-percha balls stuck to them, assuming that the fashioning of their shots required far more artistry and improvisation. The gutty had in turn replaced the 400-year-old feather ball, which got soggy when wet and was stuffed with top-hatfuls of boiled feathers. (Bear in mind that while I write this someone is firing innumerable shots not far from here.) One can guess why balls needed to be nicked and cut in order not to duck quickly in flight. Indented and dimpled balls were far more resistant than smooth-surfaced ones, which would necessarily dent when banging trees and other hard surfaces.

Speaking of birds, to see is to believe. Not wanting to soil the idea of golf as the game of eternal hope with its promised lands beyond every horizon, we'll leave out the issue about the dead blackbirds, blue jays, coots, geese, grackles, gulls, mallards, robins, starlings, widgeons and other etceteras. Without enough information to prove that the pesticides used to enhance the greens' greenness provide courses with bountiful doses of neurotoxins and mutagenic substances, why ruin people's chance to experience earthly paradise? Those 546 geese collected in a golf course in Hempstead at least can say they died in heaven. The reader should try to figure out whether snakes and rodents suffer from context disorder when the desert they dwell in is transformed into a tropical environment. *Change or die!*

Let us tread upon a course where the cardinal rule of enlightened design (and spartan, indeed) is followed: a first-class hole must present the player with an alternate route to the green.

TABLE TENNIS

—Four's too much, Ping.

—Winter's no better, Pong.

—Cut it out, Ping.

—Pull over, Pong.

—I'm on a roll, Ping.

—Stop the car, Pong.

—Three's an inch, Ping.

—Pizza pie, Pong.

—Correspond, Ping.

—Pump it up, Pong.

—Quit thinking about sad chickens, Ping.

—It's not funny, Pong.

—Almost never, Ping. Silence.

SOCCER DREAMS

O the dream, O.
What team spirit, O!
What enlightened vision of what constitutes metaphor.
Football players, yes.
When you say football you mean soccer, right?
Your players wouldn't play the other, sinister game,
a type of cancer.
Your players don't tackle.
They kick balls, O.
They must wear shorts, O.
What other games do you like?
Shooting videos? Hardly a sport.
Mud-wrestling, O?
Sumo? Guess not, it implies a balance of forces.
Kite-flying, card playing? Impure, according to you.
I've got a couple of questions, O:
if those who kick balls are called pilots,
what would swimmers be?
Sleepers.
Or maybe bombers, O.
Almost *bomberos*. Get it?
And then, what if your players switched sides,
repeating "Derose derose buth wah imrose imrose hast."
Think about it, O.
It might come up in another of your dream interpretation sessions.
How surreal, O.
And they say one of your hands can't move.
You let others do the kicking, O.
You must be proud: at night and from a distance
Ground Zero could be taken for a stadium.

DEMOLITION DERBY

Sonya is so good that all the guys pick on her, so the evening's narrative goes. I've heard she wears yellow t-shirts each time to match her hair. Last time her tennis shoes got so dusty that she had to throw them out because there was no way on earth that they could be white again.

Trunks shrink like deflated accordions, like melodramatic arguments after they've met face to face with someone's indifference. A baby cries and pouts while her mother is trying to scoop more Velveeta on to her nacho. The father is strung out on something, someone in back of us says. A teenager with severe acne turns around and fires a dart full of cavities into my gaze. We give in to the pleasure of destruction for the sheer sake of waste. What inside, the collision, the jerk on the nape that makes the driver wonder whether this one is it. Swallow me dust while the crowd cheers and claps its French fries away into the space between a nearby neon and the floodlights gathering an army of many-sized moths.

NOTES

Letter from One Practitioner to Another—"Rongi rattad ragisevad" is Estonian for "the wheels of the train roll by" and means the same as "ruedan las ruedas del ferrocarril" in Spanish. Both tongue-twisters serve the same function: one can practice the rolling of one's r's by repeating them.

How to Look at Mexican Highways—This poem originally appeared in Spanish in *Acúfenos* (Taller Ditoria, 2006).

How to Be Well Dressed: *An Intervention*—Most of this text was first lifted from the guide *How to Be Well Dressed* by Joan O'Sullivan, published by The Amy Vanderbilt Success Program for Women in 1963, and then treated.

Bite Its Heart Until It Learns **and** *Poem in Spanish*—These are my renditions of two poems ("Corazón" and "Poem in Spanish") that Paul Hoover wrote in English as if they were being written by a Spanish-language poet. My renderings are centos with lines that I found in poems by diverse Latin American authors and which I then translated into English. The lines that I selected somehow echo those in Hoover's Spanish poems because of the words, images, or ideas in them. Resulting from this "translation" project were more literal Spanish poems, in English.

Sources for *Bite Its Heart Until It Learns*
Title: Jaime Sabines, *La señal*
1–2: Sabines, "Uno es el hombre"
3–4: Salvador Novo, "Never Ever"
5–8: Vicente Huidobro, *Altazor*
9: Novo, "La parábola del ser humano"
10: *Altazor*
11: Sabines, "Entresuelo"
12: *Altazor*
13: Pablo Neruda, "Fábula de la sirena y los borrachos"
14: Sabines, "La Tovarich"
15–16: *Altazor*
17–19: Novo, "Resúmenes"
20–21: Nicanor Parra, *Nuevos sermones y prédicas del Cristo de Elqui*, LX

22–23: Parra, XLVIII
23–24: Parra, *Sermones y prédicas del Cristo de Elqui*, XXIII

Sources for *Poem in Spanish*
1–3: Huidobro, *Altazor*
4: Alfonsina Storni, "Presentimiento"
5: *Altazor*
6–7: Parra, *Nuevos sermones y prédicas del Cristo de Elqui*, XLVII
8: Alberto Blanco, "Mapas"
9: Neruda, "Entrada en la madera"
10–11: *Altazor*
12: Neruda, "Muchos somos"
13–14: *Altazor*
15–16: Neruda, "Walking Around"
17–18: Parra, *Nuevos sermones y prédicas del Cristo de Elqui*, L
19: *Altazor*
20: Salvador Novo, "Noche"
21–22: Blanco, "Los tres estados y los tres reinos"
23–24: Neruda, "Muchos somos"
25–26: Sabines, "Del mito"

To and No Fro—After *A Woman Without Love: A Family Melodrama*, directed by Luis Buñuel, 1951.

Elementary Moralities I* and *II—Raymond Queneau, founder of the Oulipo, invented this poetic form in 1973.

Bankrupt Books: A Collage—Each line in this poem is the opposite of a title in the best-seller list of *The New York Times Book Review* of April 2, 2000. The following books were featured in it: *The Brethren, A Heartbreaking Work of Staggering Genius, The New New Thing, The Greatest Generation Speaks, 'Tis, Moment of Truth, The Tipping Point, Relationship Rescue, The Art of Happiness, The Millionaire Mind, Body for Life, The Rock Says…, Eating Well for Optimum Health, Day of Reckoning, The Death of Innocence, The Bodyguard's Story, From This Day Forward, Dragons of a Fallen Sun, Carolina Moon, The Lion's Game, Shrub, The Greatest Generation, Georgiana, Girl with a Pearl Earring, Tough Cookie, Daughter of Fortune, Gap Creek, Where You Belong, Tuesdays with Morrie, The Prisoner of Azkaban, The Sorcerer's*

Stone, *The Chamber of Secrets*, *Who Moved My Cheese?*, *Peanuts: A Golden Celebration*, *Bridget Jones: The Edge of Reason*, *Have a Nice Day!* and *Beowulf*.

Convergence: A Picture Puzzle—"The world's most difficult puzzle" is taken from the essay "Jigsaw Puzzles: A Brief History" by Anne D. Williams, which was posted on the Internet. The source of the rest of the text in quotation marks is *Jackson Pollock* by Francis V. O'Connor, published by The Museum of Modern Art in 1967. This volume compiles the critical writing on Pollock's paintings published between 1952 and 1956.

Table Tennis—The poem's last line is taken from Samuel Beckett's *Ping*, although the punctuation has been altered.

Soccer Dreams—The poem is based on an article about the Osama Bin Laden videotape in which he and a group of friends appear discussing the September 11 attacks while also reciting poems and talking about their dreams. The article is titled "Dreams of Holy War Over a Quiet Evening" and appeared in *The New York Times* on December 16, 2001. *Derose derose buth wah imrose imrose hast* is Dari, the Afghan dialect of Persian, for "Yesterday was yesterday but today is today." *Bomberos* is the Spanish word for firefighters.

811.6 T635t
Torre, Mónica de la.
Talk shows